RILEY CARS
1896–1969

ROB MALPAS

AMBERLEY

Picture Acknowledgements

The pictures on the following pages were taken by the author in the following museums and are reproduced with their kind permission:

Page 5 top and centre and Page 6 centre – The Coventry Transport Museum in Coventry. Page 5 bottom and Page 6 top and bottom – The British Motor Museum at Gaydon.

First published 2019

Amberley Publishing
The Hill, Stroud
Gloucestershire, GL5 4EP

www.amberley-books.com

British Library Cataloguing in Publication Data.
A catalogue record for this book is available from the British Library.

ISBN 978 1 4456 8860 2 (print)
ISBN 978 1 4456 8861 9 (ebook)

Typeset in 10pt on 13pt Sabon.
Origination by Amberley Publishing.
Printed in the UK.

Contents

The Beginnings of a Marque 1896–1914

The origins of what was to become Riley (Coventry) Ltd can be traced back to 1851 and the birth of William Riley Junior. In 1870, he took over the family's weaving business, in which he was assisted by his brothers Herbert and Basil. Twenty years later, he had become interested in pedal cycles, and so in 1890 he acquired the nearby cycle works of Bonnick & Co. Ltd. The two companies were effectively merged in 1896, with new works being bought alongside the Bonnick works in King Street, Coventry. The Riley Cycle Co. Ltd was therefore founded on 23 May 1896 by William, who was now also working with his sons, the eldest of whom was twenty – a little older than William had been when he originally took over the business.

In 1899, the first Rileys powered by an internal combustion engine were revealed. They were a Quadricycle and a Tricycle, both called 'Royal Rileys'. They were produced by the company of Messers William, Basil and Herbert Riley – the three brothers who were shareholders of the company. These were the first official Riley cars to be offered for sale to the public. However, between 1896 and 1898, Percy Riley, one of William's sons, who was just fourteen in 1896, had developed a car of his own. The car was handmade by Percy, to his own design, in the workshops of the Riley Cycle Company; however, while it was used by the family, it was never put into full production. The car featured a number of novel ideas, but then this was the dawn of motoring, and the same could be said about many cars. However, the most important thing of note in his design was that for the first time in a car's engine, he used a mechanically operated inlet valve. Although this car was a very successful prototype, which was used for many years, it was a one-off, meaning that the 1899 Royal Rileys are thought of as the first Riley motor cars. Unlike Percy's car, these early Riley models were powered by engines bought in from other manufacturers.

Over the next few years, Riley developed the two Royal Riley designs, as well as adapting some of their bicycle designs to take petrol engines, and so become motorbikes. However, the directors were beginning to find the problems in simply adapting pedal-driven machines to petrol-driven, and so decided to design a car that was intended to be motorised from the beginning. This resulted in the 1903 Forecar, a three-wheeled vehicle with a passenger seat at the front over the axle. The Forecar, although obviously based on the motorcycles, was undoubtedly designed to be petrol-driven (as indeed was the 1903 model motorbike). It featured the first Riley-designed engine, from the Riley engine works, run by three of William Riley's sons – Percy, Victor and Allan. The engine works were situated alongside part of the thirteenth-century city wall in Coventry.

1904 Riley 3 hp motorbike. Riley launched their first purpose-designed motorbike in 1902, this example being one of the last 3 hp models from 1904, as Riley progressed to manufacturing cars.

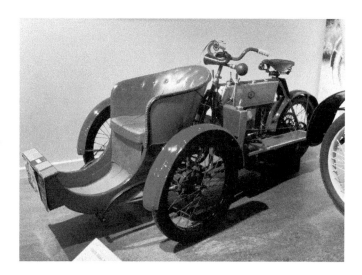

1904 Riley 4½ hp Forecar DU 458. The Forecar was launched in 1903 with a 3 hp engine, and the 4½ hp engine was added the following year. It marked the start of Riley developing car-like designs, rather than mounting engines on bicycles. It was still based on a motorbike frame, but at the front there were two wheels and a front passenger seat.

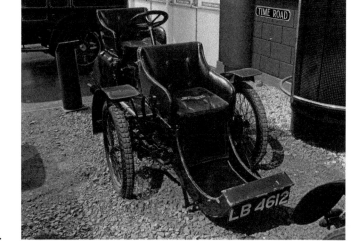

1907 Riley 5 hp Tricar LB 4612. The Tricar followed in from the Forecar, offering more comfort for the driver with a bucket seat instead of the saddle of the older model.

1908 Riley 9 YU 4031. The first Riley 9 V-Twin was Riley's first attempt at a proper four-wheeled car and immediately proved successful, encouraging the brothers, if not their father, into further development of motor cars.

1908 Riley 12/18 SWB Tourer NS 105. The 12/18 hp was available with two wheelbases, and a vast array of body styles. Sadly, there are very few survivors – only two are known in the UK – and little idea of how many were originally built.

Riley 10 hp AB 1390. Ultimately replacing the smaller 9 hp, the 10 hp was a scaled down 12/18, with the V-Twin engine mounted at the front and a range of body styles available.

Two years later, the 1905 Tricar, a development of the Forecar, was the first Riley to use a steering wheel in preference to handlebars. It also had some form of bodywork and started to look less like a converted motorcycle, with the driver's saddle replacing a bucket seat, like that already used for the passenger in front, and a platform for the driver to rest his feet. These 9 hp Riley Tricars were the first to enter motorsports, and their success eventually led to Riley's interwar domination of their class in many races. Over the years, the Tricar design was developed significantly, until it ended production in late 1907 due to the introduction of more modern four-wheeled Rileys.

Since 1905, a 'proper' four-wheeled Riley car had been under development and was ready for production towards the end of 1906. The development of this car had led to the Riley Engine Co. having to move over the summer, with the aid of a lorry that they specifically built themselves. It was able to carry up to 2 tons, simply using the V-twin 9 hp engine from the Tricars. The factory also built other small lorries, both for their own use and for other local businesses who saw the value of such a vehicle. However, Riley never put a commercial vehicle into regular production. The new car was a light two-seater, also using the V-twin engine, and available with an optional hood. Throughout 1906 and 1907, the cars were successful in many of the sporting events (including many hill climbs) that they were entered in, winning a large number of them outright, although often this was due to handicapping procedures in place.

A significant development that Riley used on their cars was the patented detachable wheel, which meant that the puncture didn't have to be repaired in situ as the wheel could simply be replaced. Early cars had used solid rubber tyres, but as pneumatic tyres came into common use, the need to deal quickly and efficiently with punctures grew. This wheel was another important development by Riley in the history of the motor car, and the idea of the knock-off hub on a wire wheel is still very much with us. Indeed, by 1914 Riley were supplying wheels to around 180 other car companies.

Another sideline developed by Riley at this time was the supply of engines to other companies for a variety of industrial and commercial applications. Perhaps the best known of these are the Tasmanian Railcars, which were built between 1904 and 1907 and used Riley engines, and other components, as their motive power. Some also used chassis built by Riley. One of these small railcars still survives, having been restored by the Don River Railway in Tasmania. The success of these railcars also saw an order for a similar system in South Africa, but by contrast little is known about these.

In late 1907, Riley had decided that a larger car to complement the successful 9 hp model was necessary. Therefore, they developed the Riley 12–18 hp. This still used a V-twin engine, but scaled up to about 2 litres. The car was usually a four-seater, but had many different bodies put on it in its lifetime, both by the factory and by outside coachbuilders. These bodies included a landaulette, two-seater, and four-seater with rearward facing rear seats. Most models featured tool trays under the front passenger seat, an idea that was used on many further Rileys (although later transferred to an under-bonnet location). By the 1908 motor show, another new model had been launched in the shape of the Riley 10 hp. This was generally a two-seater model, with a shortened chassis and a smaller engine than the 12–18 hp on which it was based. Most of the development of the Riley cars was now being carried out by William's sons, with Percy responsible for the engines and running gear and Stanley the body design. The other family members played lesser parts as controllers of the various Riley companies. The success of the cars led the Riley Cycle Company to cease production of bicycles by 1911.

During 1910, the 9 hp model was gradually phased out, leaving the company running a two-car production line. Then, through 1913, many changes were made in the company infrastructure. The Riley Motor Manufacturing Co. took over car production, at new works next to the Riley Engine Co., and the Riley Cycle Co. changed its name to Riley (Coventry) Ltd and concentrated on the patented detachable wheels. Much of this reorganisation was caused by William's sons wanting to pursue the manufacture of cars, while he himself was more cautious and saw the cars as a novel sideline, with the main business strengths in the smaller machines and wheels. However, in the long term his sons got their way and he relented. During this period of reorganisation, a brand-new car, the Riley 17 hp, was launched. It was the first Riley to feature a four-cylinder engine, although at 3 litres it was the largest Riley engine ever built. Again, various bodies were available, but production hardly got under way before war was declared. Although the slogan had been in use for some time, the larger, more powerful 17 hp model was the most worthy of Riley's advertising line – 'The King of Cars'.

The Early Models 1914–25

At the end of 1913, Stanley Riley returned from a world tour, and transferred his attention from the successful Riley Motor Manufacturing Co. to another Riley company, the Nero Engine Co. Ltd, which Victor Riley had founded some time earlier. He almost immediately started work on a new 10 hp engine, and then a new car to carry it, as a sort of replacement for the discontinued 9 hp. The car was finished later in 1914, but the outbreak of war stopped any real production, with just a handful of cars apparently produced. In 1916, the Nero Engine Co. bought some land at Foleshill, on the edge of Coventry, to further the production of war materials. After the war, this site became the new headquarters for Riley, replacing the many small, cramped and old workshops and offices in the centre of the city. However, the larger Aldbourne Road site, first acquired in 1906, was retained.

Straight after the war, Riley underwent further reorganisation, with Riley (Coventry) Ltd ceasing production of wheels and absorbing the Nero Engine Co. and the Riley Motor Manufacturing Co. They all moved out to the new factory site at Foleshill. It seems that neither the 1908 10 hp nor the 12-18 hp models were put back into series production after the war, meaning that until a new car was developed, Riley's only car on the market was the 17 hp. Production of this model was continued by the Riley Engine Co. until 1921, when the horsepower tax was introduced, which made it too expensive for many potential customers. During this time, the company also produced electric lighting systems, and engines and equipment for boats, the latter continuing until 1926 and sporadically thereafter.

Back in 1918, a new company based at the old Riley Motor works, called the Midland Motor Body Co., was set up under Allan Riley. Their initial aim was to produce a new model fit for post-war Britain, and it was ready for launch at the 1919 motor show. The first new Riley was the 10.8 or 11 hp, bearing for the first time the now famous 'V-radiator', and diamond badge. The cars' chassis were made at Foleshill, before being transported to the Midland Motor Body works to have the bodies lowered into place. The bodies were either three- or four-seaters, and could be removed fairly easily while still leaving all of the mechanical and electrical components in place. This car continued for several years, and in 1920 it was the first Riley to be marketed with the slogan: 'As old as the industry,' which was later appended with '… as modern as the hour.'

1923 Riley 10.8 two-seater coupé HP 6433. This rare surviving example of a Riley 10.8 carries two-seater coupé bodywork of a type that developed into the Ascot body of the early 1930s.

1924 Riley 10.8 Redwing Tourer HP 9679. This was another surviving 10.8 Riley, although this time thought to carry a non-standard body, with four-seater touring coachwork. The colour scheme is that used for the famous Riley 'Redwing' sports models of the early 1920s, although they invariably carried two-seater coachwork.

1925 Riley 11.9 Coach FY 8825. The four-door Coach model was one of the more upmarket bodies Riley offered on the 11.9 chassis. Although not designed as a full chauffeur-driven limousine, it offered comfortable family transport, with a fully enclosed body that was not so common in the mid-1920s. Although there was no luggage boot, a fold-down rack could be mounted over the spare wheel to carry luggage.

By 1923, the bodyshop had also been transferred out to Foleshill, where further land had been acquired to accommodate the growing factory. In the same year, the Riley 10.8 was treated to a wide range of improvements and renamed as the 11/40, with considerable successes made in many of the racing events that Rileys entered. Most were private entries, but several were aided by the Riley companies. Two years later, in 1925, the 10.8 engine was enlarged to produce 11.9 hp. Customers now had the choice of either engine in their cars, and the split was roughly 50/50 with all bodies, except the two-seater. This car (unofficially known as the Redwing due to its polished aluminium body with red wings) generally had the 10.8 hp. However, despite the successes that these models were gaining for Riley, the company had decided that a new model must be developed. The designs for the new 9 hp engine and chassis were finished in 1925, and the first few cars were built in early 1926. This was the now famous Riley 9.

Building on Success 1926–31

The Riley 9 prototype, with Monaco bodywork, was first unveiled at Shelsey Walsh in 1926. It aroused great curiosity as, unusually for small cars of that time, it was fitted with closed saloon bodywork. Furthermore, the body was covered with fabric, which was still seen as the preserve of more luxurious models. The engine was completely new, with overhead valves for the first time. Another novel feature on small cars was the integral boot at the back of the car. By the 1926 motor show the Riley 9 was fully developed and several bodies (including the Monaco) were on show, alongside a supercharged 11/40 and the 'new' 12 hp, which was basically just a renamed 11.9 hp. The Riley 9 entered full production in early 1927, with a slightly revised Monaco body, or tourer. Later in 1927, two further bodies were made available – a two-seater tourer with dickey seat, and the San Remo four-seater saloon.

The year 1927 was also an important one with regards to Riley's sporting heritage, as it was during this year that the sporty Brooklands was first raced. It had been developed by J. G. Parry-Thomas and following his untimely death the work was completed by a team led by Reid Railton. The car was an immediate sensation, with outstanding performances up and down the country. It was based on a short 9 chassis, with a shorter radiator set behind, rather than on top of the front cross members. The narrow passenger compartment was sunk between the chassis rails and the rear axle was underslung, with the chassis members swept up over the axle beam to create a low car that was much more aerodynamic than many others of the day. In total, over 100 Brooklands models were produced, with many of their innovations finding their way into passenger cars and larger racing models in the coming years. During 1928, the Riley 9s managed to set many new speed records, and win many races, mainly due to the excellent performance of the Brooklands model.

For 1928, Riley dramatically improved the now ageing 12 hp with a modified engine and new bodies. These were all now given names, rather than just descriptions, to bring them more in line with the new 9, which had by now been christened as 'The Wonder Car'. The main bodies on the 12 hp were the Lulworth, Chatsworth and Grangeworth saloons, and also the Wentworth Coupé. However, this was the model's swansong, as the success of the Riley 9 led to the demise of the old side-valved 12. At the end of 1928, it was replaced with the all-new 14/6. This was a 1,633cc, 14 hp, six-cylinder car. In general appearance, the car was very similar to the popular 9, but it was larger in all dimensions.

The car first shown featured fabric bodywork and was called the Stelvio, with Weymann coachwork resembling the Monaco. In addition, the more traditional metal-bodied Deauville saloon and Special fabric tourer were launched shortly afterwards. At the same time, the Monaco 9 was slightly improved, with a bigger, wider boot, and a new Biarritz 9 was introduced. This featured a one-piece bonnet, hinged at the rear instead of the then more common centre-hinged, sideways-opening bonnets, albeit with lift-out side panels to improve access. Between 1926 and 1929, over 6,000 Riley 9s had been produced, with demand still high for the exceptional cars. Despite being an increasingly old design compared to much of their competition, they were still winning many races at the end of 1929, and continued to do so throughout the 1930s.

> Our native automobile engineering industry contains one or two examples of undertakings owned by a single proprietor. For the rest, with one exception motor-manufacturing companies in England are publicly owned. The unique case is that of Riley, which has always been, and remains in effect, a family concern...
>
> From the preface of *The Riley Romance*, by Edward H. Reeves, Jan. 1930.

This statement probably helps explain the success that Riley found – the fact that it wasn't run by a single person, or by a board of squabbling directors, but by a family who all had roughly the same ideas for the company.

Despite only launching one new model in 1929 – the 14/6 6-light saloon – Riley had a very successful year. This was also true on the track, with many new lap records being set, as well as many wins at the races that the Riley team entered. The racing success undoubtedly helped lead to a record £1,000,000 of sales – quite some feat for a small company in the 1920s!

In 1930 Riley introduced an all new 9 'plus' range. This comprised the Monaco and Biarritz saloons, Brooklands Sports, open four-seater tourer and two-seater coupé with dickey seat (which was later renamed the Ascot). The 14/6 range also underwent modifications, with the 6-light and four-seater tourer being refreshed and renamed as the Alpine and Alpine Tourer respectively. The more upmarket Stelvio saloon and Sportsman's coupé were also updated. The success of Riley in motorsport continued and was further improved with the new 9-plus. In addition, the Riley engines were made available to the new Brooke-Riley motorboats, which proved a popular success for the Riley Engine Co. Late in 1931, another new model was launched in the shape of the WD or Army tourer. This was a civilian version of the Riley 9 tourer model proposed for use by the War Office, although few of either were built. The 1932 range was launched shortly afterwards and comprised seven bodies on the 9 including the two-seater Gamecock sports. These models also saw a further improvement to the engine and chassis, which was now called the 9 Plus Ultra. However, the 14/6 stayed much the same, with just the Alpine and Stelvio models. The end of 1931 marked William Riley's eightieth birthday, and also saw Riley (Coventry) Ltd taking over the Riley Engine Co. and the Midland Motor Body Co., so that all of Riley's production was now carried out by the one company.

Above and below: 1927 Riley 9 Brooklands VC 485. This historic example of the Brooklands is still in regular use on tracks up and down the country. There is some confusion in its history, however, with a Brooklands-based special built by John Treen carrying the same registration number. Nevertheless, this car is believed to be a genuine Brooklands model.

Above and below: 1930 Riley 9 Brooklands VC 8305. Believed to be one of the last of the Brooklands models, this was one of a batch registered by the works racing team in 1930 and used in various events before being sold on. It is, however, still used in competition today.

Above and below: 1927 Riley 9 Australian Special BF 8528. In the early years, few complete Riley cars were exported, and especially in Australia bare chassis were bodied and trimmed locally. This is one such car, only recently returned to the UK, and carrying two-seater plus dickey coachwork, not unlike Riley's own Ascot model.

Above and below: 1928 Riley 9 Clay Castle Special UU 8996. This car is another example of a chassis carrying a period body from an outside coachbuilder, in this case Clay Castle in the UK. The long tail houses a large top-opening luggage space, but the car is a strict two-seater.

Above and below: 1930 Riley 9 Special Tourer GJ 1209. Although originally launched as a fabric-bodied model, by the 1930s fabric bodies were going out of fashion, and so Riley offered a steel-bodied variant of the tourer. The following year, the design was substantially changed, meaning this was one of the last of the original tourer models with the older, narrow radiator and more upright appearance.

Above and below: 1931 Riley 9 Monaco OY 1353. The Monaco started life as a fabric saloon with room for four and a luggage boot behind. This 1931 model has the chassis upgrades of the Plus series Monaco, which also saw the boot extended to the full width of the car. The Monaco continued to sell well for Riley, accounting for a large proportion of their overall sales at the beginning of the 1930s.

Above and below: 1931 Riley 9 Drophead GG 7524. The drophead was a long-running model that carried various names over the years. This example is a 1931 Drophead Coupé, with the latest Plus-Ultra chassis upgrades, but still featuring the dickey seat behind the hood. There is also a clever compartment under the hood for storing umbrellas.

Above and below: 1932 Riley 9 Ascot UYJ 224. In late 1931, the old drophead model was updated and renamed as the Ascot. It still featured two seats and a dickey seat behind, but as dickey seats fell out of fashion, sales dwindled and so the Ascot was abandoned in favour of newer models. The body was also available on the six-cylinder chassis, although it seems very few were produced.

Above and below: 1931 Riley 9 Biarritz OY 83. The Biarritz Silent Saloon was launched in 1928 and initially it was a full fabric saloon, but later became half-panelled. While similar in shape to the Monaco, there were many differences between the two, including a split rear window and a one-piece, full-width rear-hinged luggage boot. Moving forward, there were roof ventilators and the front doors and bonnet sides met without the more normal scuttle panel between.

Above and below: Riley 9 WD Tourer HX 6507. This car is owned by John Lomas, owner of Blue Diamond Riley Services, and has been fully restored and kitted out for entering the 2015 Monte Carlo Rally. The car excelled on this epic challenge and has also competed in other events. The WD Tourer was originally conceived as a car for the Army, but despite a handful of cars being trialled, there is no record of a final order. The model was also made available to the public, but few are thought to have sold.

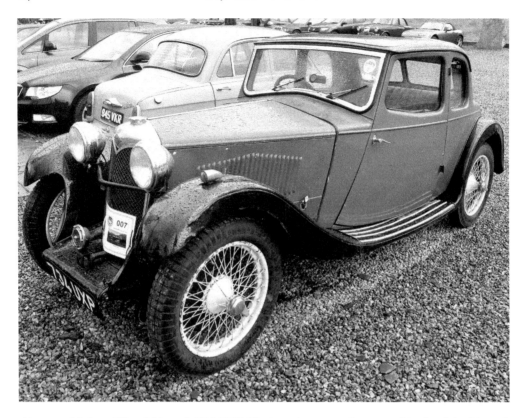

Above and below: Riley 9 Lincock 734 UXP. The low-slung two-door coupé body of the Lincock has a very sporting appearance, quite different from most other Riley models at the time, which were either open or four-door saloons. This particular example is in regular use, and therefore not restored to concours condition, despite its rarity.

Above and below: 1932 Riley 9 Gamecock CG 555. Launched in 1932, and only available for just over a year, the Gamecock was a two-seater open tourer with a large luggage boot. Not as sporty as the earlier Brooklands, nor as practical as the later Lynx, it was nevertheless a strong seller in its short life. This particular example carries a 12/4 engine transplant. The diamond shape of the rear window and bonnet side vents can be seen on this car. This became a common motif on Rileys in the early 1930s.

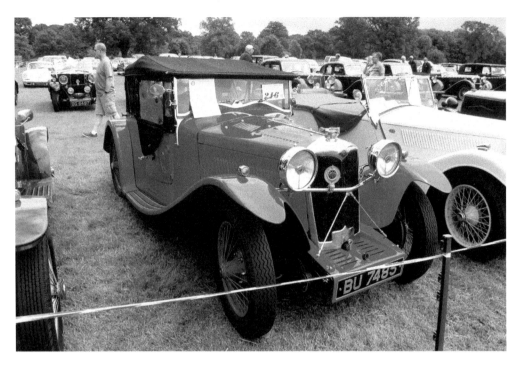

Above and below: 1933 Riley 9 March Special BU 7485. The March Special was named after Lord March, who played a part in its development. It sat between the full sports models and the more sedate tourers such as the Lynx. There were small occasional seats in the rear, and behind them a large fuel tank and twin spare wheels suitable for long distances, but without a luggage boot it was perhaps more a rally car than a grand tourer.

Above and below: 1933 Riley 9 Monaco OC 8836. In late 1932, an all-new Monaco body was launched. There was no longer a fabric-bodied option, and the sharp folds of the aluminium give the car a much smarter appearance than the softer curves of the fabric. A reshaped boot and rear doors hung from the rear completed the makeover, with the Monaco remaining Riley's cheapest and therefore bestselling model.

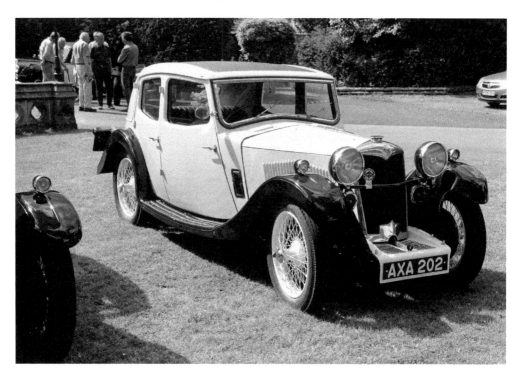

Above and below: Riley 9 Kestrel AXA 202. The Kestrel stood out from the crowd on 1930s roads, where many cars were still boxy and upright, and was also loved by its owners for the fine handling and sporty qualities, all at a competitive price.

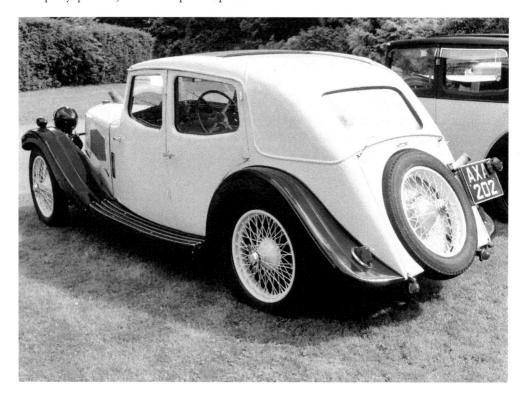

Riley 9 Kestrel BPE 903. To many people, the Kestrel is Riley's finest saloon-car design, and the revised 4-light version of the body is the best of the bunch. The 9 chassis never received the new 6-light version of the Kestrel, leaving the 4-light on the market until late 1936. Certainly, while many other Riley models have dwindled over the years, whether scrapped or converted into a special, the Kestrel has survived in much greater numbers.

1934 Riley 9 Kestrel AHU 58. This car spent many years residing in the author's shed, before being reluctantly sold in 2016 due to moving house. Many of the components are carefully balanced on the car in the photos to give an impression of a complete vehicle, but in truth it had been substantially dismantled in a long-abandoned restoration effort. It is hoped that the new owner has more success.

Above and below: Riley 9 Lynx HS 7336. When first launched, the Lynx had a two-door design with disappearing folding hood. This folded away into a compartment behind the rear seat, with a cover over the top, much like modern convertibles only without any automation! Pitched as a more sedate tourer than some of the sportier open models, the car nevertheless enjoyed the fine handling characteristics of the 9 chassis.

Above and below: Riley 9 Lynx BLM 667. For 1934 the Lynx was improved with four-door coachwork, but the novel disappearing roof was discontinued in favour of a more traditional hood that sat on the rear of the car. The hoods still retained the diamond-shaped rear window, reflecting the Blue Diamond badge, a motif reflected in many other details such as door handles and embossed on filler caps.

Above and below: 1934 Riley 9 Imp KV 8932. The Imp was a scaled down version of the MPH racing models, but unlike some of the intervening sports models since the Brooklands, the Imp was a proper racing car, designed to be equally at home on road or track. Although this example is a genuine Imp, the ongoing popularity of the model has led to a large number of replicas being produced over the years.

Above and below: Riley 9 Merlin DTW 222. The Merlin was conceived as Riley's route into the mass market, with the bodies being supplied complete by Briggs and simply fitted to the Riley chassis, thus speeding up production and reducing costs. However, while the car was a good seller, the volumes did not increase sufficiently for the optimistic contract, forcing Riley into further adaptations.

Above and below: Riley 14/6 Alpine Tourer GT 5989. Originally known simply as the Tourer, the Alpine name was added in 1931 to associate the open car with the renamed saloon. The model had been a traditional fabric-bodied four-door, four-seater at first, although steel-bodied models accounted for the majority of production by the 1930s. It was later replaced by the Lynx, an all-new, low-slung tourer.

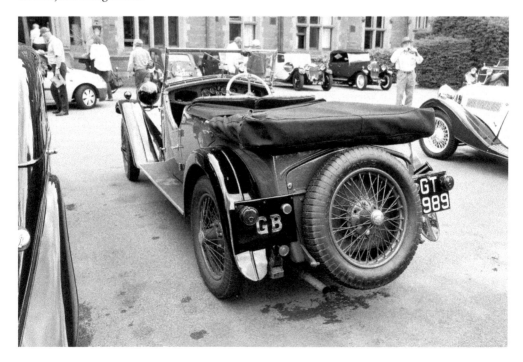

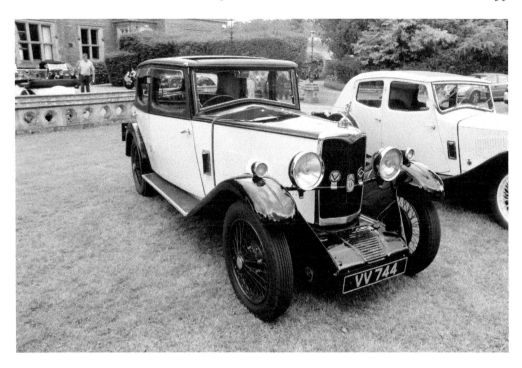

Above and below: Riley 14/6 Alpine VV 744. The Alpine Saloon was a new model for 1931, replacing the old 'six-light saloon' and styled like a large Monaco. It was an instant success, selling more than the other existing saloon models, and surviving until the 14/6 engine was phased out. The body was now half-panelled, with steel below the waist and a fabric top. Most Alpines sported a nice little enamel badge on the radiator showing a skier and 'Alpine 6'.

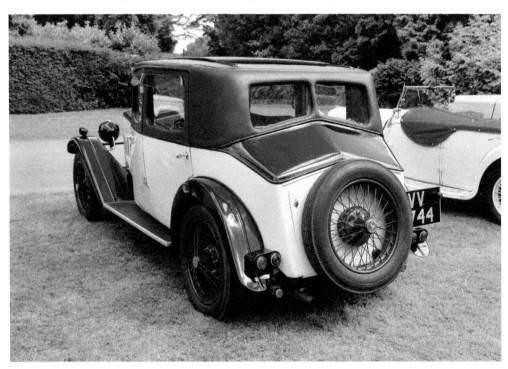

Above and below: Riley 14/6 Deauville PL 8617. The Deauville is one of many larger saloons built in small numbers by Riley in the early 1930s. Sadly, most survive in single figures, if at all, but this nicely restored example shows off the fine coachwork that was produced by Hancock & Warman for Riley. Production ceased in 1931 after the coachbuilders suffered a major fire.

Above and below: Riley 14/6 Alpine Gamecock ADU 27. Although carrying the original registration, this particular car is a faithful replica of the original Alpine Gamecocks, which were built in the 1980s by Barry Gilles who then owned one of the genuine cars, ADU29. At least three of these cars were originally built by the factory in 1933 to compete in a range of competitions and were either rebuilt or followed by another batch in 1934.

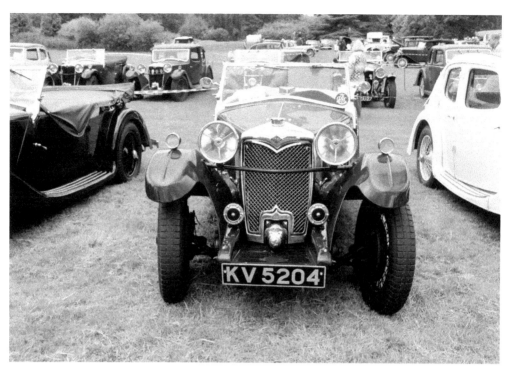

Above and below: Riley 14/6 Lynx KV 5204. The original Lynx was a two-door model as already described on the 9 chassis. The 14/6 Lynx later became a four-door model, which sold even better than the original model. Replacing the four-door Alpine Tourer, it carried over some styling cues, including the cut outs in the front doors, despite being a much lower-slung model.

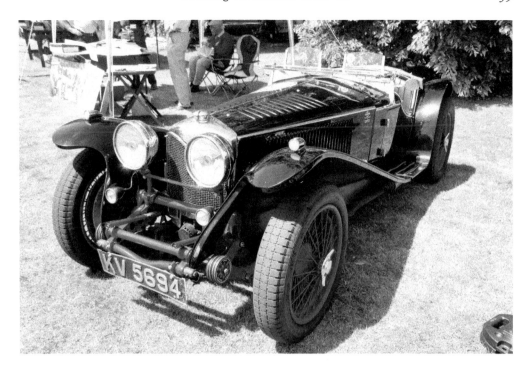

Above and below: 1934 Riley 14/6 MPH Prototype KV 5694. This car was one of two prototype MPH models produced in early 1934, using the chassis and running gear of the previous year's six-cylinder TT racing car. This car was used in publicity for the new model, raced, then later experimented with by ERA, and still competes today. No more than two dozen MPH models were ultimately built, including racing models, with only about a dozen survivors.

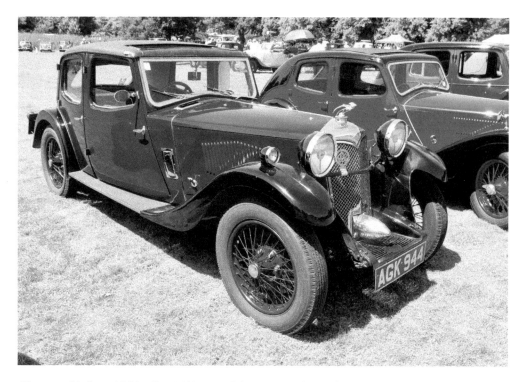

Above and below: 1933 Riley 14/6 Kestrel AGK 944. This early Kestrel is a fine example of the early body shape, with the sunshine roof and snub tail. The chromed 'bullet' protruding from the radiator is not, as is sometimes thought, a supercharger, but the dynamo. However, Riley were no doubt content to let people think it was a supercharger!

Above and below: 1934 Riley 12/6 Mentone ST 7775. The Mentone was designed to sit between the Monaco 9 and Alpine 14/6 as the 'standard' saloon in the new 12/6 range. As such, it shared many design similarities with the other models, offering a smart four-door saloon with steel or fabric bodywork. There is still a profusion of diamond motifs in the styling and detailing of the car.

Above and below: 1933 Riley 12/6 Kestrel HV 2680. This is one of the earlier 12/6 Kestrels, showing the stubby tail design of the early cars. Nevertheless, the Kestrel was a very stylish design when launched, with few competitors producing a car on such rakish lines. There were further updates the following year to keep the model at the top of the market, such as different, integrated running boards and an all-steel roof.

Above and below: 1934 Riley 12/6 Kestrel APP 166. The longer sweeping tail of the 1934 Kestrel body is clear to see when compared with the earlier design (opposite). The earlier fabric-coated roof has also been replaced with an all-steel roof, which could now be specified in a range of colours, although most were black when they left the factory.

There's no Stopping Riley! 1932–36

Following on from winning the 1,100cc class in the 1931 Monte Carlo rally, nine Rileys were entered in the 1932 event. The previous year's winner came third overall, with other Rileys gaining fourth and fifth places. This was just one of the many rally successes of the era, not to mention the Grand Prix events. During 1931, the plant at Foleshill was enlarged again, partially in order to start export production. Rileys could already be found across the empire, and indeed many other countries in every continent. However, the Riley company itself hadn't yet exported a single car. Instead they either relied on approving local importers who would order cars from the factory for customers or, in places like Australia, sent out chassis in component or CKD (completely knocked down) form for local completion, including local parts and, more often than not, locally built bodies as well.

Later in 1932, the 'new' 14/6 engine was adapted to make the slightly smaller 12/6 engine. The idea behind this was that the engine would then be eligible for the under-1,500cc class in motorsport. The first few cars with this engine were fitted with larger Brooklands-style bodywork, and mainly used in trials and races. By the end of the year, however, the 12/6 was available to the public. The new engine option coincided with the launch of a number of new body styles across the range. This meant that the Riley range now consisted of nine Riley 9s, including six new models: the four-seater Kestrel and Falcon saloons, the Lynx four-seater tourer, the Lincock two-seater coupé, March Special and two-seater Trinity tourer.

The 14/6 range also underwent some changes, with the Stelvio and Alpine continuing, while the new luxurious Edinburgh five-seater limousine was launched along with the Winchester, a slightly more moderate version of the car. Most of the 9 hp bodies were also now available with either of the six-cylinder engines, although the Monaco equivalent on the 12/6 chassis was called the Mentone, as the bodywork had to be adapted more than the others to fit. Despite this, it seems unlikely that some of the bodies were ever actually produced on the larger chassis, except perhaps as a prototype or demonstrator model. As with many car manufacturers of the era, these options were available to boost the apparent range in the brochures, but if someone actually wanted to order one, attempts would often be made to steer them to another model that was already in production at the factory.

By mid-1933 the Riley Motor Club had become the largest single-make motor club in the world, with over 2,000 members. Its history dates back to 1925, making it one of the oldest single-make clubs still in existence. From the start, the club had the full backing of the Riley family; indeed, some of the brothers held positions on the club's board. While the club continues to exist and cater for all Riley models, the more specific Riley Register (for all pre-1938/9 cars) and RM Club mean that the Riley Motor Club now has a large number of BMC Riley owners amongst its membership.

In mid-1933, Riley started public testing of another new car – the MPH. This car was in many ways a six-cylinder Imp, and apart from a longer bonnet and a different tail style, it looked nearly identical. The MPH was based on the running gear of the successful TT Sprite models, which had been designed for the TT races and then used in various sporting events over the previous year. Other prototypes and specialist racing models were built around this time, some of which were raced regularly while others were quickly cannibalised for the next project. Many of these cars would compete in different classes in different events, with the engines being swapped between all three of the available six-cylinder units to suit (and later also the 12/4 engine). It is therefore very difficult to give a definitive answer as to how to restore a car to its original factory specification!

For 1934, many improvements were made across the range, but the only all-new car was the Imp. This was a two-door, two-seater sports tourer, essentially intended to succeed the long-departed, but still successful, Brooklands. The Kestrel and Lynx were also modified in appearance, as were the Mentone and 14/6 Stelvio. In addition, all of the closed saloons were now metal-bodied, as opposed to fabric, and it was the same for the fabric-bodied tourers. Over the years, the popularity of fabric-bodied cars had waned. Originally seen as a more upmarket solution than plain steel, it subsequently became the bodywork of choice for a number of small cycle cars, thus cheapening the image. Riley had adapted over the years, with half-panelled models – i.e. steel below the waist line – coming to market from 1932, and all-steel alternatives following soon after.

At the same time as the successes experienced by the Riley works team, there were a number of privateer teams on the racing circuits. Freddie Dixon is perhaps the best known entrant, with his Brooklands-based Red Mongrel and later Dixon Specials, which were based on the 1933 works TT cars. Two of these specials and another Brooklands model are still competing in period events. However, perhaps of even more importance was the formation of ERA, or English Racing Automobiles, late in 1933. Founded by Humphrey Cook, Raymond Mays and Peter Berthon, the first car was the so-called White Riley, itself based on another 1933 TT car and developed by Raymond Mays. The success of this car led to the creation of ERA, which used many Riley components in their subsequent models, a staggering sixteen out of twenty of which survive, most still in use on track.

For 1935 another new engine was launched – the 12/4. This was a completely new design, and the first not to be designed by the family, although it bore many resemblances to the existing Riley engines. It quickly replaced the 12/6 in the middle of the Riley range, as the older engine lost demand to the new 1½ litre engine. This new chassis featured a completely new Falcon body, which later replaced the existing Falcon throughout the range. There was also a modified Kestrel body at launch, although there is some doubt as to how quickly the Kestrel was put into production. The Lynx tourer body was also made available later in the year, with the later four-door design replacing the original two-door model. In addition, the 14/6 engine was replaced with a new, larger 15/6, which took all of the standard bodies, as well as a revised Stelvio. However, as became typical with Riley, both the 12/6 and 14/6 engined models remained available as a special order.

The big news, in terms of Riley's history, in 1935 was the new contract with the Briggs bodies company of Dagenham to supply pre-built steel bodies to the factory. Up until then, Riley cars had predominantly featured hand-formed aluminium bodies on ash frames, so this was a significant departure for the company. The idea was to increase production at a lower cost by sub-contracting the work, while also producing a stiffer body. However, unfortunately, after some initial success, the plan backfired and towards the end Riley were trying ever more desperate ways of selling the stockpiled bodies. It is not known what minimum volume the contract agreed upon, although a figure of 5,000 has been suggested, perhaps over the span of a two- or three-year contract (at the time full annual production was only around 5,000 cars). However, at the end, when Riley called in the receivers, they had a large number of stockpiled bodies, while dealers were struggling to sell the cars they already had. In total around 3,200–3,300 Briggs-bodied cars were produced over the three years. This body was launched as the Merlin on either the 9 or 12/4 chassis, and later also used for the more luxurious Falcon, on which the design was originally based. Later, in 1937, a larger boot was added to create the Touring saloon, while the original body was retained for the basic 1938 Victor.

Racing successes still abounded for the Riley teams, and for many races, Rileys were the cars to beat in their class. However, 1935 saw the start of the withdrawal by the factory team, Riley focussing instead on supporting the many private teams who were running competition Rileys. Therefore, after over thirty years of competition successes, entries by the factory came to an end.

Above and below: 1935 Riley 12/4 Falcon CPE 426. The Falcon was the first body launched on the 12/4 chassis, and for several months it was the only body available as Riley battled against problems on the Kestrel and Lynx. As such, it was by far and away the bestseller. Although not as rakish as the Kestrel, the Falcon was nevertheless a stylish choice in a market place which still had some very square, boxy and upright competitors.

Above and below: 1935 Riley 12/4 Lynx CMG 384 and CGH 397. Unlike the models already looked at, the 12/4 Lynx was never fitted with the two-door body. Instead, it had the new four-door body from the start. The Lynx was the last of the bodies made available on the 12/4 chassis in its first year, but was a strong seller when it did arrive.

Above and below: 1935 Riley 12/4 Kestrel AVE 6. The sporty Kestrel saloon was a natural choice for the new 12/4 chassis, the powerful new engine matching the styling and handling of this Riley design. For the first year the body featured the original 4-light design with the longer swept tail that had been introduced the year before, albeit slightly revised. Previously the coachline had crossed under the rear window, but for the new 12/4 body, the lines were swept down the tail above the rear wings.

Above and below: Riley 12/4 Lynx CKO 838. This particular Lynx is sporting the full glass side screens and tonneau cover that were available from Riley, all in a matching colour to the hood. The horns and headlight grilles were also period options. While most models received straight bumpers, those fitted to the Lynx were shaped to fit around the curvaceous wings.

1938 Riley 12/4 Lynx Sprite JTR 512. This is another concours condition Lynx, with many of the period options that were available for the car, including radiator mascot, horn and badge bar, at the front. As with the other models, the Lynx was treated to some extra chrome in 1937, with a new radiator grille and straighter bumpers as standard. This particular car is fitted with the Sprite engine, giving higher performance from the twin carburetors and other detail improvements.

Above and below: 1936 Riley 12/4 Kestrel AKV 892. For the 1936 models, Riley completely redesigned the rear of the Kestrel bodywork again to create a 6-light design. The shape of the side windows was also adjusted to give a straight coachline, losing the slightly diamond-shaped windows of the older models. The cars were also now available as Sprite Series, with twin carburettors and a higher level of tune better matching the stylish coachwork.

Above and below: 1936 Riley 12/4 Kestrel Sprite CVC 127. The 12/4 Kestrel was one of Riley's biggest sellers over the years and had many detail changes in addition to those already noted. Again, this car is fitted with the Sprite engine. The following year, 1937, all cars including the Kestrel were fitted with chrome, vertically slatted grilles ahead of the radiator, spare wheel covers and also large full-width chrome bumpers became standard front and rear.

Above and below: Riley 12/4 Sprite EMB 136. The Sprite was a sports car produced by Riley from a collection of parts. It used the same basic chassis structure as the MPH models but was fitted with the newer 12/4 engine. The body, too, was similar to the MPH; however, by fitting the cowled radiator cover at the front, Riley completely changed the look of the car. This example is race-trimmed with cycle wings and small aero screen windscreens.

Above and below: Riley 12/4 Sprite BCR 810. This Sprite carries the perhaps more familiar enclosed wings and full-size windscreen that were supplied with the road-going models. Although most would probably have left the factory looking like this, the Sprite was and still is a popular track car.

Above and below: 1936 Riley 12/4 Falcon AWU 580. Despite the new Briggs body being based on the Falcon design, for 1936 Riley still built the traditional body for the Falcon. Yet again, there were delays in getting the new bodies into production, so the Falcon remained a strong seller for the first few months before the Adelphi took over as the big seller in the range.

Above and below: 1937 Riley 12/4 Falcon ASC 962. For 1937, the Falcon shared its steel, Briggs-built body with the Merlin. Unfortunately, however, the Falcon was perhaps not different enough from its cheaper brother and sales plummeted. As a result, it is now one of the rarer models, and was replaced the following year with the Touring Saloon, sometimes erroneously called a Falcon, even when being sold from the dealerships.

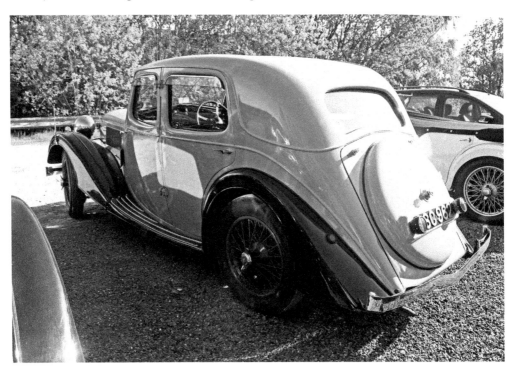

Above and below: 1937 Riley 12/4 Adelphi DZ 3737. The Adelphi was launched as the new mass-market Saloon with new 6-light coachwork, which is quite different to previous Riley models. Indeed, in some quarters it was considered rather staid and ordinary when set next to models like the Kestrel with their flowing lines. Nevertheless, it proved to be a good seller on the 12/4, 16/4 and V8 chassis – it accounted for most of V8 production. There are fewer survivors, however.

Above and below: 1936 Riley 12/4 Adelphi CUV 146. The colour scheme of this Adelphi is perhaps more authentic, but more anonymous than the car opposite. The 6-light notchback styling was a departure for Riley, and provided the basis for the interim 1939 models after the Nuffield takeover. They, however, are even rarer than the Adelphi.

Above and below: 1936 Riley 12/4 Merlin YXG 543 and BFG 207. The Merlin was launched for 1936 as the new 'bottom of the range' Riley. This was achieved, in part, by buying in completed bodies from Briggs in Dartford. Unlike the hand-built aluminium over ash frame bodies used on other Rileys, these bodies were based on the previous year's Falcon design, but all steel with the relative benefits and pitfalls. The Merlin was also available on the 9 chassis.

Above and below: Riley 12/4 Continental CAO 134. The Continental was another completely new model from Riley, and only available for a single year on the 12/4 chassis. The Continental name was quickly dropped, the model rebranded as a Close-Coupled Saloon, supposedly due to complaints from Bentley who were already using the name. Today it is one of the rarer and more sought-after models.

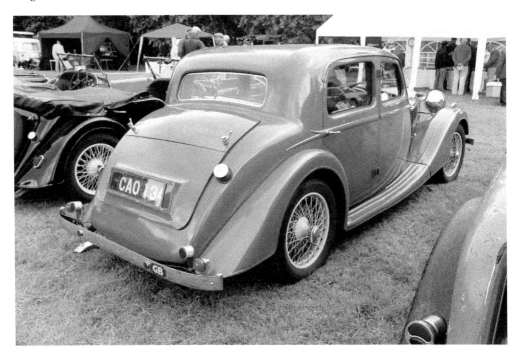

Above and below: 1937 Riley 12/4 Touring Saloon ELH 135. There is no denying that the stylish lines of the Touring Saloon look good, but unfortunately buyers at the time were not convinced. An attempt to fit the body to the larger 16/4 chassis was even less successful, and it is doubtful that more than one finished car was ever built. Most survivors, therefore, are 12/4 models.

Above and below: 1938 Riley 12/4 Touring Saloon EYE 942. As a perhaps desperate attempt to make the body contract with Briggs work, Riley requested the design be changed a little to feature an extended boot at the back. While this provided a larger luggage space, the access was no longer so easy, being reduced to a small hatch at the top in place of the whole tail opening.

The End of the Era 1936–39

The year 1936 saw some major changes to the Riley range, with a modified Falcon body and the new Merlin intended to replace the 9 hp Monaco and 12 hp Mentone as the 'base' model. In addition, a new V8 engine was introduced, and many of the lesser models were dropped. The range now consisted of twenty-three models, ranging from the 9 hp Merlin and Kestrel up to the V8 Kestrel and Adelphi models. In between were the 12/4 Merlin, Kestrel (now 6-light), Falcon, Lynx and new Adelphi models and the larger 15/6 with Kestrel, Falcon, Lynx, Adelphi or MPH bodies. Many of the models in the range were also available as 'special series' (making the twenty-three), an idea which was launched in around 1930 and basically consisted of uprated suspension, engines and gearboxes to give a sportier feel to the car. Extra body features were also included. The 8/90 V8 engine was essentially two 9 hp engines placed at 90 degrees to each other and sharing a common crankcase, although it was not quite that easy to develop. It was not a success, and only about twenty-five are believed to have been built. In addition, Riley later launched the all-new Sprite, a two-seater sports car with streamlined front end and the 12/4 engine.

The following quote, from Riley themselves, sums up the problems that were to follow: '...we make far too many models of course. But then we have a pretty fertile design department, and we like making nice, interesting cars.' (Riley advertising, September 1936)

For 1937, the Riley Monaco reappeared, although with very different styling. The new design was very similar to the larger Adelphi, and was the only 6-light body ever produced on the 9 chassis. In addition, the Kestrel 9 and Merlin 12/4 were discontinued as Riley tried to consolidate and simplify the range. All models now had bumpers, trafficators and interior lights (even the tourers). Throughout 1936/7, the sporting excellence of Riley cars continued; although fewer outright wins were recorded, they were still a marque to be reckoned with.

Late in 1936, a new marque, called Autovia, was launched in Coventry. One of the company's directors was Victor Riley and the engine and gearbox were obvious developments of those used in the Riley 12/4 and 8/90 ranges. Although not a Riley, the Autovia shared too many design features with Riley models to be generally regarded as a completely new or different car. The only completely new Riley model for 1937 was the Continental touring saloon, on the 12/4 chassis. By mid-1937, Riley had also completed development of its all-new 2½ litre four-cylinder engine. This was intended to be the new range-topper in place of the unsuccessful V8 8/90 and older six-cylinder models and was called the Big-Four. The new Big-Four was available with Kestrel, Adelphi, Touring or Close-Coupled Saloon bodywork and the Lynx tourer, although the first two accounted for the majority of sales.

For 1938, with the advent of the new Big-Four engine, the range was drastically changed again, with the demise of the existing 9 and 15/6 models. This left Riley essentially with a two-engine line-up of the 12/4 or 1½ litre and 16/4 or Big-Four. Both were available with Adelphi, Kestrel, Lynx, Continental or Close-Coupled saloon and touring bodies, with the 12/4 also available as the Sprite sports model. However, despite the availability, only one Big-Four Lynx was ever produced, and the touring saloon body proved so difficult to mount on the larger chassis that it is not known if any cars left the factory, despite up to three prototypes being thought to have existed.

The Adelphi could also still be bought with the 8/90 or 15/6 engines direct from the factory, although it seems that few were ordered. It is also interesting to note that the Sprite was the only real sporting model left in the range, despite the continuing success of Rileys on the track. All models now had a radiator grill, with vertical slats mounted in front of the traditional honeycomb radiator, and the bonnet louvres had been removed. Bumpers were standard on all saloon models, both front and back, and so were steel covers for the spare wheels. In addition to the models listed above, a brand new 12/4 or 9 hp Riley, the Victor, was launched at the motor show. This was the cheapest Riley model and was the last outing for the 9 engine.

In November 1937, at the AGM, the first hint of financial trouble was sensed outside the company with the announcement that the previous eighteen months' accounts were to be rigorously checked through. By February 1938, a merger with Triumph was rumoured but at the end of the month Victor Riley, the Chairman of Riley (Coventry) Ltd, announced that the receivers had been called in. The many attempts to reduce expenses that the receiver made included closing the London spares depot, liquidating the bodies branch and Riley Engine Co., and selling off all Riley shares in Autovia (a significant amount). This financial difficulty led to a dramatic drop in staff, and therefore production levels. However, privately entered Rileys still performed exceedingly well in many of the races that they took part in. Cars were still leaving the factory, built up from bodies and parts that were there, creating a few cars with interesting technical differences. Many of the cars produced at this time used the Briggs bodies, of which there had been a substantial stockpile.

By September, rumours of a takeover by Lord Nuffield had been confirmed. He stated that: 'Lord Nuffield in acquiring the Riley Organization is desirous of preserving in every way the development of those characteristics that have made the Riley car so outstanding.' Immediately after purchasing Riley, Lord Nuffield resold it to Morris Motors for £1, so as to improve the company's financial position. The company was then renamed Riley (Coventry) Successors Ltd, with Victor Riley appointed Managing Director. Lord Nuffield made it clear that the company could continue as before, with financial backing from Morris Motors. However, many detail changes were made to the cars still being assembled, including some parts being replaced with standard Morris stock to reduce cost but not affect Riley performance or style. Shortly after the takeover, Morris Motors became the Nuffield Organisation, now comprising Morris, MG, Wolseley, and of course Riley.

Things then happened very quickly, and after a brief hiatus in production when the only cars sent out from the factory were previous orders and new vehicles still using up the stock of old parts, a new range was launched. This consisted of a 12 hp saloon and drophead as well as a slightly larger 16 hp saloon and drophead. Thus Riley had gone from a bewildering array of models to just four, all with components taken from the Morris parts bin, and yet still retaining those Riley engines that endeared the marque to so many people. These two bodies were designed in-house by Riley, albeit under Morris supervision. Therefore, the saloon model is a clear development of Riley's own Adelphi body, and the drophead was simplified as a two-door convertible version of the saloon, rather than trying to define its own style like the Lynx had done.

The range was soon expanded due to popular demand, however, with the return of the Kestrel. Only available on the 16 hp chassis, this was the last of the old Riley models to be produced. Despite the impending war, this small range of Rileys proved surprisingly successful, with in the region of 750 12 hp models produced, and over 100 16 hp models, before production finally ceased early in 1941.

The changes in 1938 also meant the final demise of the Riley 9 after well over 25,000, and perhaps as many as 30,000, had been built since 1926. Shortly after the 1939 range was launched, however, the Foleshill plant, like so many others across the country, was turned over to war production, and while a few cars continued to trickle out of the works, it was no longer the company's priority. It was during the Second World War, in 1944, that the founder of Riley Cycle Co., William Riley, died. He had outlived his own company, which had survived for forty years and produced some of the most outstanding cars of its time.

Above and below: 1938 Riley 16/4 Continental AUN 917. The Continental, or Close-Coupled Saloon body was also fitted to the 16/4 chassis for the final year of the independent company. The alternative name arose from the seating layout, which featured less rear leg room than normal in order to provide a larger boot. The theory was that the target market was dashing young couples, perhaps with a young child or two, who sped across the Continent on expensive holidays! It is still a large and imposing model.

Above and below: 1938 Riley 16/4 Kestrel RLY 16. The new Big 4 engine was an important addition to the Riley range, and perhaps in different circumstances it could have been Riley's saviour, but unfortunately they had spent too much money on developing too many models. All of the cars featured the later chrome grilles, bumpers and also a 'Blue Streak' motif on the bonnet sides as a quick identifier of the new models.

Above and below: 1941 Riley 16/4 Kestcock Special GGK 581. This special has been constructed on a Riley 16/4 Kestrel Saloon's cut-down chassis, but the damaged body has been replaced with a two-door coupé style, retaining some of the shape of the original saloon. The Kestcock name merges 'Kestrel' with 'Lincock' – Riley's own two-door coupé available on the 9 chassis in the early 1930s.

1937 Autovia Saloon CRW 709. The Autovia Project was another drain on Riley's limited finances, even if it was nominally a separate company. As an attempt to move into the luxury market, the cars produced were of high quality and had the presence on the road to match, but the marque never had time to find its feet before Riley called in the receivers. In addition to this elegant Saloon, there was also an even more opulent Limousine model. There are a large number of survivors today out of the forty-four cars believed to have been produced.

Above and right: 1940 Riley 16 Kestrel EVC 880. Following customer requests, Nuffield reintroduced the Kestrel body on the larger 16 hp chassis in mid-1939. There were many detail changes to the car since the 16/4 model. Steel wheels replaced the traditional wire wheels, the 'Blue Streak' bonnet motifs were gone, and the car featured all of the chassis updates of the new Saloon and Drophead.

1939 Riley 12 Drophead GGT 775. The new 'Nuffield' models for 1939 saw the Riley range trimmed down to a saloon and drophead available on either the 12 or 16 hp chassis. The saloon was a development of the Adelphi, and the drophead a roofless, two-door version of the saloon. Compared to the sleek lines of the Lynx, the drophead was rather upright and lacking much of the Riley charisma.

The RM Years 1946–57

After the end of hostilities in May 1945, car manufacturers around the country were eager to get new models rolling off the production lines and into showrooms. Nuffield was no exception. However, with Riley the 1939 range was considered 'ancient and outdated', having been designed as a mere stopgap until new Morris/Wolseley-based products could be launched. War had put paid to this idea, but fortunately there was still some life left in the old 1½ litre and Big-Four engines. As such, a new chassis had been developed during the war, almost in secret, using traditional techniques, and an ash-framed body designed to cover it. An early decision was made to use different wheelbase lengths for the two engines, as with the prewar 12 hp and 16 hp models, and so different length bonnets, although the bodies were identical from the A post back. The first of this new design was the RMA, which was launched in late 1945. After the slight interruption in design terms of the immediate pre-war models, these new Rileys shared many styling cues with their more illustrious forebears. There are clear similarities with the short-lived Continental or Close-Coupled touring saloons, and also with the well-loved Kestrel.

For the immediate post-war period, the RM series was as fresh in design as was possible; most manufacturers were still churning out their 1939 models, and some were relying on even earlier designs. However, the design, quality and handling of the new RMs were something to behold. The RMB was launched in early 1946 and was even more desirable, with the longer bonnet and more powerful engine. Post-war shortages meant that production figures remained low, and that many of the cars that were built were exported. However, there were a few customers across Britain who were able to get hold of new cars, and the magazine reports of the day raved about them.

By 1949, the RMC (three-abreast roadster) and RMD (four-seater drophead) had been launched, both on the larger engine RMB chassis, and the RMC at least was aimed squarely at the American market to aid the export drive. However, neither fared well, either overseas or at home, and they were dropped in 1951 after only around 500 of each had been built – today they are the most valuable of all RMs. There were also many specials built by outside coachbuilders, including 1½ litre dropheads, and estate cars, or woodies. The factory also produced some specials, with a period photo showing a 6-light limousine model in the works. The RM series succeeded in being a well-built, stylish and desirable luxury saloon, with the larger engine model capable of nearly 100 mph. However, it failed in that few people could afford such a car after the war. By the time production had increased enough to meet demand, the Morris Minor was about to be launched at half the price of the cheapest RM, and so providing motoring for the masses. The Riley RM was therefore always a middle-class, aspirational model.

By 1952 the RM was starting to feel dated alongside the newer rivals that had been launched, and so revisions were made to create the RME and RMF. The original plan was to revise both the mechanics and the styling in one go; however, with the advances being made by other manufacturers, and the recent formation of BMC, things got pushed along a bit. This resulted in the mechanical revisions being introduced in October 1952, and styling twelve months later. However, the 2½ litre sales were slow, even with the revisions, so the newly formed BMC decided to replace the RMF with an entirely new, Wolseley-based model – the Pathfinder. Nuffield had already developed this car as a potential Riley, sharing much of the design with the Wolseley 6/90, while retaining the Big-Four engine and running gear, but it was BMC that completed the development.

The history of Riley cars between 1952 and 1955 is very muddled; there are lots of conflicting rumours and ideas that unfortunately cannot be confirmed for sure. As was explained above, the RME and RMF were launched in 1952, being mechanical revisions of the RMA/B. However, before the formation of BMC in early 1952, Nuffield had already started the development of the next generation models. These were to be the RMH Pathfinder and the possible RMG model. A rumoured RME replacement, based on the Wolseley 4/44, the RMG, is still unconfirmed, but the coding of the Pathfinder as RMH is a clear suggestion that the RMG code was left clear. There is also some evidence to suggest that the name Wayfinder or Wayfarer was intended for the model. It is not at all clear why development of this model was halted. With the formation of BMC, the RME/F was hurried through without the styling revisions that were planned. BMC then further hurried the launch of the Pathfinder to try and counter the RMFs slow sales. However, in all this confusion the rumoured RMG falls out. Whether it ever left the drawing board is unknown, but perhaps unlikely.

The new Pathfinder was essentially a Wolseley 6/90 with Riley Big-Four engine and gearbox fitted. BMC also fitted a traditional Riley grille on the front and a Riley-style interior. It was jovially known by its owners as the Ditchfinder and seemed to get off to a good start, the more modern, full-width styling proving popular, but sales dropped away. BMC had launched the car after stating their new engine policy, which would consign Riley's Big-Four to the graveyard. The fact that the Pathfinder still used it was an ongoing, expensive problem.

At the same time, the RME received the long-planned facelift, which is still controversial among RM fans. The big visual differences were that the running boards were removed and spats were fitted over the rear wheels, both of which meant that the front and rear wings were redesigned. However, there were also a large number of detail changes, not all of which were introduced at the same time. The car was also laden with extra chrome and many 1950s design 'features', such as windscreen visors, were available as extras. The RME was finally discontinued in 1955 after disappointing sales, and eventually replaced with the all new 1.5 in 1957.

Meanwhile, the Pathfinder soldiered on alone until 1957, when it also received a facelift, with a slightly updated bodyshell and a BMC C-Series engine finally replacing the Riley Big-Four. In a mere five years since the formation of BMC, they had effectively wiped out the marque, stripping it of all its heritage, leaving the Pathfinder as the last true Riley.

Above and below: Riley RMA HYX 975. The Riley RM was one of the first brand-new British cars to be launched after the Second World War. First released in autumn 1945 as the 1½ litre (the RMA code, as with all of the RMs, was a factory code not widely known until after the BMC takeover in 1952), the car was warmly received by public and press alike. Its stylish lines, mated to the renowned Riley engine, made it a highly desirable car through the late 1940s.

Riley RMA LYB 886. Much of the charm of the new RMs lay in the effortless blending of vintage and then-modern aero styling. The full wings, faired-in lamps and wide body produced a stylish car with roomy accommodation and sufficient power to keep up in traffic. The new slogan of 'Magnificent Motoring' certainly fitted well with the new RMs.

Riley RMA FKV 817. The earlier dashboard design seen in an RMA. The three round dials were later replaced with more modern-looking rectangular units, as seen on the RME.

Above and below: Riley RMB LKK 875. Launched in spring 1946, as the 2½ litre, the RMB is distinguishable from its little brother by the longer bonnet to accommodate the bigger engine, and pale blue in place of dark blue badges. The larger engine also gave it more performance, with a top speed in the mid-nineties. As with the RMA, post-war rationing and export requirements meant few were sold in Britain for the first couple of years.

Above and below: Riley RMB ASN 530. Many of the early RMs left the factory in austerity black, just like this one, and while some of the two-tone schemes owners have since applied can be a little garish, black is not the best colour for showing off the elegant lines of the RM. Nevertheless, it is still a common colour, which was also favoured by the police, with many constabularies using RMs in the 1950s.

Above and below: Riley RMC YXG 911. Riley developed the Roadster model for the American market, hoping for large volumes of exports. However, perhaps due to the somewhat ungainly appearance, in the end about as many were sold in the UK as the US, and after three years and just 500 sales, the model was dropped. The car featured three-abreast seating on a narrow bench seat with column shift, later adapted to two seats with a standard shift for UK tastes.

Above and below: Riley RMC 2+2 Special KXF 332. The provenance and origins of this car are uncertain, but it has been well finished. The space behind the front seats has been extended to fit small occasional rear seats, and the hood has also been extended to suit. This gives a much more balanced appearance to the car, with the rear deck being considerably shorter. There are rumours of a similar car being produced in the factory, but never put into full production.

Above and below: Riley RMD JYV 959. The RMD kept much more faithful to the original RM shape than the RMC, and as a result appears to be a much better proportioned car. It also had the benefit of being able to carry four or five adults in comfort. Sadly, however, the buying public were less convinced than Riley fans of today, and so as with the RMC, production lasted for just three years and around 500 examples.

Above and below: Riley RME PJH 580. The RME may have been visually little different from the RMA, but mechanically there were many improvements. The traditional torque tube was replaced with an open propshaft, and brakes and engine were uprated. It wasn't enough, however, against the newer competition, and so styling changes were carried through just a year later. Over the years subsequent owners have improved the car's lighting in many varied ways, some more successful than others.

Above and below: Riley RME CHF 693. The creased front wings and faired-in sidelights can be seen on this RME. At the rear, later models had the rear lights moved to the wings, as so many owners have done since, with a separate number plate light added. While two-tone bodies were common, a single colour could still be specified – although many RMs have been repainted over the years in colour schemes of their owner's choice.

Riley RME JJN 664. The revised RME models from 1953 featured many styling changes to try and reinvigorate sales, the majority of which were to the wings and running boards. The addition of spats over the rear wheels certainly made the car look very different to its predecessors, but the jury is still out as to whether it was an improvement. The revised dashboard layout of the later cars can also be seen (middle). Although introduced in 1949/50, it was then retained unchanged until the end of production in 1955.

1952 Riley RMF GFO 994. The RMF was the last, and in many ways the best, of the RM series cars. Mechanical changes to the running gear meant that the car was now capable of an indicated 100 mph, just, and Continental trials proved its reliability and that it could carry passengers and luggage effortlessly across Europe. Sadly, BMC had other ideas, and with sales slow the RMF only lasted in production for just over a year.

1952 Riley RMF MHP 816. This car belonged to the author's father through his childhood and he has many happy memories of travelling across the south and west of England attending car rallies and events. It was later resprayed in green.

Above and below: Riley Pathfinder 951 UXP. This particular Pathfinder may be looking a little tired around the edges, but it is a fine example and still in regular use. Although using the engine, gearbox and some other mechanical parts from the RMF, the new Pathfinder, or RMH, shared a lot more in common with the Wolseley 6/90. The bodyshells were nearly identical, and sadly this car marked the end of Riley's individuality.

The End of a Great Marque

The year 1957 saw great changes for Riley. The last car that could be described as carrying any Riley heritage, the Pathfinder, was shelved and replaced with a full Wolseley clone. The 2.6 was essentially a Series II Wolseley 6/90 with a different radiator grille and badges. The engine was a tuned version of the BMC C-series 2.6 litre 'Six', which was used in the Wolseley and also the large Austin and Morris saloons of the time. The interior was also largely the same as the Wolseley, and apart from extra speed in the Riley, the two cars handled the same as well.

That same year the delayed and much smaller replacement for the RME was launched. Originally intended to be a Morris Minor replacement, the car was adapted with more luxury appointments to provide both Riley and Wolseley with a new small model. Called the 1.5 by Riley, and the 1500 by Wolseley, it was again essentially a Wolseley with a different radiator grille, tuned engine and different trim. However, the car sold extremely well, beating all other Riley models' production figures with over 30,000 cars built! It seems that even after two years with just a single model on the market, the demand for Rileys was still there, and the launch of the 1.5 saw a renaissance in Riley's sales, even if the cars were not necessarily to the taste of the diehard fans.

In 1959 the 2.6 was discontinued after just 2,000 had been built, roughly a quarter of the total Riley and Wolseley production. It was nominally replaced by the 4/68, the Riley version of BMCs ubiquitous B-series Farina models; however, this was a smaller car with less power and it seems that no one was fooled into thinking it was a real successor to the big Rileys of old. It was powered by the same 1,489cc B-series engine as the 1.5, but due to the larger, more roomy body and heavier weight, it had less performance. As a result, it appealed to a different market, and the two were sold alongside each other. It was replaced by the 4/72 two years later, which had the larger 1,622cc B-series engine introduced earlier in the year but never fitted to the smaller 1.5. This car soldiered on until the death of Riley in 1969, albeit with miserable sales figures and stiff in-house competition (primarily from Wolseley and MG).

Also launched in 1961 was the Riley Elf. Again, this was a cosmetic job on a Wolseley model, this time the Wolseley Hornet, itself based on the Mini. The Elf was another good seller for Riley, offering the well-loved handling of the Mini in a more upmarket package. In many ways it was a worthy successor to the Riley 9 of the 1920s and '30s but it wasn't enough to keep the marque alive. 1965 saw the end of the 1.5, when it was replaced by the smaller Kestrel 1100 A-series Farina model, again another cross-BMC car. The reuse of the Kestrel name was controversial, with many people seeing it as a cheap way to cash in on the heritage of what they considered to be a much better car. Nevertheless, the new car sold well, and the sharp handling of the range, coupled with the luxury appointments of the Riley model, meant it was much closer in essence to the Rileys of old than the larger 4/72 model. The car was updated in 1967 as the Kestrel 1275, then quickly renamed the 1300. This model was fitted with the larger 1,275cc Mini engine, giving more power. The 1100 stayed in production for a short period, but was phased out in 1968 and the 1300 was discontinued along with the Elf, 4/72 and the Riley marque in July 1969.

Riley's demise was caused by a variety of factors, which included the falling sales, the lowest of any of the mainstream marques in the new British Leyland group. There were also many complaints against BMC rubbishing Riley's heritage with a range of lacklustre saloons. The huge financial troubles experienced by the new British Leyland Motor Corporation (from the merger of BMC, Jaguar-Daimler, and Leyland (Rover/ Triumph)) meant that money was tight and resources had to be targeted to where there was a potential profit. There was therefore a lack of funds for new models for so many marques, and sadly Riley was the first casualty. There was also a lot of perceived competition between Riley, MG, Wolseley and Triumph's models. These all combined to force BLMC to kill off the Riley marque. It was the first of many, however; within the same twelve months Austin Healey also went, and by 1975 Wolseley had followed.

Riley Two Point Six SNR 970. The 2.6 was much more closely aligned with the contemporary Wolseley 6/90 models. Out went the Riley engine, replaced with the BMC C-series six-cylinder engine and gearbox, complete with column shift. The bodies were also brought in line with one another.

Above and below: Riley 1.5 257 STF. Although it hides it well, the Riley 1.5 is based on Morris Minor parts, with the larger B series engine fitted. While this led to a cramped four-seater cabin, it also produced a small, agile car which is often still seen on the track at classic racing events. Updates over the years made detail changes to the body, but the overall shape remained unchanged for nine years of production.

Above and below: Riley One Point Five 711 GOW. To many people's eyes, this car needs restoring, but as the old saying goes, if it ain't broke, don't fix it! It is certainly refreshing to see a well-used and well-loved old Riley still on the road which hasn't been restored to concours condition, and of course there would have been many more like this on the roads in the 1970s when these Rileys fell into 'Banger' territory.

Above and below: 1967 Riley 4/72 JAF 18E. The 4/72 arrived in 1961 as a thorough mechanical update of the 4/68 model. Featuring a wider track and larger engine, the driving experience had edged closer to what was expected of a Riley, but was still a far cry from their heyday. Nevertheless, the car sold steadily at first, before trailing off in the later 1960s. A prototype 1800 (Landcrab) with Riley grille was created as a replacement, but never put into production.

Above and below: 1969 Riley 4/72 MDM 137G. As a car of the 1960s, the 4/72 was laden with chrome from nose to tail, and all sorts of extras were available, such as hoods for the headlamps, sun visors for the windscreens and wind deflectors for the doors. When coupled with some of the more extreme two-tone colour schemes available, the result can look somewhat flamboyant to modern eyes, but fortunately the cars pictured here are relatively standard.

Above and below: 1966 Riley Elf Mk II GNT 996D. The Mk II Elf enjoyed detail updates from the original model, not least of which was the larger 998cc engine, but it was the Mk III (opposite) that gained the visible updates of integral door hinges and wind-up windows, features not given to the Mini itself until 1969 when production of the Elf came to an end.

Above and below: Riley Elf Mk III 7537 LZ. One of the last Rileys, the bodyshell of the Elf had changed little since it was introduced in 1961, the integral door hinges being the most noticeable difference, but under the skin was the larger 998cc engine and improved mechanicals, and for the passengers there were wind-up windows as well as other improvements to the cabin. All this made the little Elf a very desirable car.

Above and below: Riley Kestrel PNT 410G. The Kestrel 1275, later officially renamed as just the Riley 1300, was the last new Riley to be introduced in 1967 and was sold for just two years before the Riley marque was discontinued. Although not always to the purists' taste, it was by no means the worst of the BMC Rileys and, as with most of the BMC 1100/1300 range, it is now a sought-after car, admired for its handling and packaging.

Riley's Legacy

Looking back through Riley's history, it is clear that the motoring world has much to thank this small Coventry firm for: from the mechanical valve operation of Percy's first car to the detachable wheels that proved so successful before the First World War. As the years progressed, Riley pioneered new ideas in body design, producing low-slung sporty cars and also experimented with new gearbox ideas such as the pre-selector and overdrive. Not all of these ideas were unique to Riley, but they were often at the forefront and without their developments, proving that the ideas could be put into production and sold successfully, the history of car design could have been very different.

From 1938, however, Riley steadily lost its independence as the parent company grew larger and more unwieldy. Its demise was, in many ways, inevitable and while some are grateful that the marque wasn't applied to any more models unworthy of the badge, most Riley fans mourn the passing of this great brand. This was certainly true for former BMW Chairman Bernd Pischetsrieder. In 1994, BMW acquired the rights to Riley as part of their purchase of the Rover Group, and over the next few years Riley was back in the news as one of the brands that BMW would have liked to resurrect. The primary idea seems to have been a coupé version of the Rover 75, and there were even models, or mock-ups shown. However, Bernd's time in charge was cut short and the new management saw some of his plans as frivolous, so even before they abandoned Rover itself, the rebirth of Riley had been shelved.

When Nuffield took over in 1939, they did not acquire all of the family companies. As noted above, Autovia had already been sold, and while no further cars were produced, the company remained active in supporting Autovia owners. There was also another Riley subsidiary that avoided Nuffield's takeover. This was PR Motors, the old Riley Engine Co. which Percy Riley, and later his widow, retained ownership of until the 1960s. It survives to this day as a subsidiary of BI Engineering in Birmingham, called PRM Newage Transmissions.

In addition to the companies, some of the factory sites occupied by Riley over the years are still in industrial use. Most of the small inner-city works have been demolished and redeveloped over the years, the Luftwaffe undoubtedly playing a role in this process. However, the early works in Aldbourne Road still stand, and were home to PR Motors until they relocated to larger premises in 1974. The buildings are now used by NDE Clarke-Pitchline, a manufacturer of gears and transmission equipment. The later works at Foleshill also still stand and are home to Unipart Powertrain Applications, another business within the automotive industry.

Unsurprisingly, Rileys remain popular cars today, well loved by the many people who have come into contact with them over the years. This means there are thriving clubs both in the UK and across the world, supporting thousands of owners in their love of these beautiful cars. Compared to some of their contemporaries, pre-war Rileys enjoy a high survival rate, although this is not evenly spread. With a rich racing heritage, the sportier models survive in far greater numbers than the more mundane saloon cars and are highly sought after. This extends to the point where over the years many end-of-life saloon bodies have been stripped and the running gear reused to create a replica of one of the sportier models. Nor does this always apply to replicas; since at least the 1920s, people have been building their own bodies on Riley running gear, creating a vast array of 'specials', some of which are now bearing replicas of their own.

To find out more about Rileys, why not visit the author's website at www.rileyrob.co.uk?

1930 Riley 9 Special MY 6775. This little two-seater model uses one of the earlier Riley 9 chassis, and as such it is not known what bodywork the car originally carried. However, this is a post-war rebody which appears to use a shortened chassis.

1934 Riley 9 Special OW 4095. This special is recorded as having been built on a life-expired Kestrel 9 chassis. The bodywork is reminiscent of the Imps, but is perhaps a little longer. The car is well used in competitions, as intended.